DUAL CITIZENSHIP

The Christian and Politics

by

Patrick Matrisciana

with D.A. Miller

Jeremiah Books

Hemet, California

Printed in the United States of America.

Dual Citizenship
Patrick Matrisciana

Cover Art - Tim Ramos

ISBN 1-878993-66-6

Published by:
Jeremiah Books
P.O. Box 1800
Hemet, CA 92546

PREFACE

Our God is the author of absolutes, yet within well-defined boundaries. He allows choices unique to each of us. All too often though, we Christians transform these personal choices into a rigid list of rules. In so doing, we negate the "moment by moment" leadership of the Holy Spirit. This legalistic perversion surfaces in many areas of our lives, including the arena of our responsibility toward government.

One extreme side of the spectrum reveals politically active Christians, dedicated to a particular cause, who condemn believers for not participating in their marches, boycotts, letter writing and other methods of political protest. Christians not actively joining the "cause" are sometimes even challenged as not being genuine believers.

Then, in complete contrast to the activists, we see Christian leaders who distance themselves from all political activity. They teach that the world's problems will only be solved by spiritual answers and that Christians have no place becoming involved in secular government. They quote scriptures to the activists about obeying government authorities and praying for leaders (hinting that politically active Christians are lawbreakers who never think to pray for government officials). Although these leaders adamantly proclaim their "always obey the government" doctrine in free nations, they fail to explain how Christians living under evil totalitarian leadership should respond to unjust government.

This dilemma is as old as man. It springs from our dual natures (both physical and spiritual), which produce citizenships in an earthly, physical country as well as the invisible spiritual domain.

Most believers in Jesus Christ recognize their spiritual responsibilities of living righteously and declaring the gospel, but the ancient dilemma remains. Should

Christians become involved in the secular world of government in order to advance moral causes and promote a better climate in which to deliver that gospel, or should they just allow the focused preaching of the gospel to naturally correct ethical wrongs and produce the more favorable environment?

Dual Citizenship explores these concurrent citizenships, seeking to outline the biblical guidelines of responsibility toward both. I believe the solution lies somewhere between the two extreme views cited.

CONTENTS

CHAPTER 1

THE ANCIENT DILEMMA: SECULAR VS. SPIRITUAL

In 1877, James Garfield, the twentieth President of the United States, gave warning to the American people. "Now more than ever before, the people are responsible for the character of their Congress. If that body be ignorant, reckless and corrupt, it is because the people tolerate ignorance, recklessness and corruption. If it be intelligent, brave and pure, it is because the people demand these high qualities to represent them in the national legislature." He continued, "If the next centennial does not find us a great nation...it will be because those who represent the enterprise, the culture, and the morality of the nation do not aid in controlling the political forces." [1]

President Garfield understood his dual citizenship. As a citizen of America, he served as a teacher, a college president, a major general in the Union Army, a congressman for eighteen years and finally as President (until he was assassinated in office).

His spiritual citizenship as a Christian prompted a life-long commitment of daily Bible reading, preaching and active opposition to slavery.

We live at the end of that next centennial about which President Garfield spoke. Have those 100 years ended with Christians standing up for justice and truth by "demanding high qualities in those who represent them"? No, they have not. Unfortunately, those 100 years have seen Bible-believing Christians slowly abdicating responsibility in secular affairs, allowing immoral leaders to take control of the arts, education, media and government. The retreat from positions of leadership occurred early in this centennial, particularly because of Christians' theological overreaction to "modernism." The move toward modernism alarmed Bible-centered Christians. They observed the doubt produced by its "higher criticism's" ridicule of doctrinal absolutes and biblical accuracy.

These modernists, in harmony with their disdain for the established fundamentals of the faith, preached a "social gospel." Since they taught that mankind was basically good and needed only a better environment in order to become "good Christians", their gospel centered on helping people physically. The government, in concert with religion, was supposed to implement this improved environment. The modernist doctrine of salvation involved changing people from the outside-in rather than the orthodox theology of regeneration from the inside-out.

Christians who desired to bring people back to the fundamentals of the faith and who rose in protest against the creeping spread of modernism were dubbed "fundamentalists."

The Christian fundamentalists' firm stand against modernism and its social gospel subtly prompted Bible-centered

Christians to back away from all governmental involvement. Their abdication of leadership positions meant that biblically-based Christians no longer led in industry, science, communication, art and politics as they once did. They not only surrendered their historic dominance of governmental leadership, they also withdrew from mandated Christian responsibility, even giving over care of the poor to the government.

Throughout the twentieth century, Bible-believing Christians gradually retreated into their spiritual cocoons of correctness, isolating themselves from their earthly citizenship and its responsibilities.

This produced disasterous results. Now today, as a whole, we Christians have become so busy "preaching to the choir", staying pure and combating modernism that we overlook the example of Jesus, who walked among the people, spoke out against corruption and cared for the hurting.

We have forgotten the biblical

admonition to live **in** the world, but not be **of** the world. Remember, God used kings and servants, statesmen and fishermen, doctors and tentmakers—to lead, to reprimand, to exhort and to serve—each using their professions as springboards to relate the glorious message of faith towards God.

Many Christians have set aside those biblical examples. Instead they come together in insular Christian communities, safe from the "pollutions" of the world, satisfied in having their own needs met while ungodly leaders continue advancing their "social gospel" to a lost and hurting world.

I also see resignation of earthly responsibility being reinforced today by some Christian leaders. Even some highly respected evangelists and pastors teach that our only focus must be our heavenly citizenship, and that secular responsibility is confined to being law-abiding citizens and praying for our political leaders. They reason that since the Bible teaches that all powers are ordained of God, we would be blocking God's will to criticize or speak against leaders, even if we personally disagree with their policies.

Other Christians believe that dual citizenship mandates responsibility in local and federal politics as well as responsibility to the kingdom of God. Israel is used as an example of a nation whose government began with this premise. These Christians point to prophets in the Bible who spoke up against ungodly leaders, holding them accountable to God and to the populaces over which they ruled.

Most concede that before Jesus came, God used prophets to call leaders to accountability when they had sin in their lives or were leading people in a path contrary to God's laws. But some dismiss these examples by saying, "That only occurred in Old Testament times" or "That only applies to the nation of Israel." But we can't dismiss the ministry of prophets as being only "Old Testament" when we consider the ministry of John the Baptist. Consider the boldness of this prophet about whom Jesus said, *"There is not a greater prophet than John the Baptist."*[a] When Jesus spoke these impressive words, John was in prison for **speaking out publicly against the immoral behavior of Herod, the local Roman political leader.** Shortly afterward, Herod executed John—this greatest prophet of all.

Although John's primary ministry was telling people to repent and prepare to meet Jesus, he lost his life because he spoke out against evil in the life of a government official. Neither the Roman government nor Herod claimed to be followers of Jesus Christ, but John still took a stand against the evil in Herod's life. John's example of speaking out against immorality in the life of a secular leader was in accordance with godly principles. This we know because God, who never changes, recorded His will

---

[a]Matthew 14:1-12; Luke 7:28

for us on this matter. *"Have no fellowship with the unfruitful works of darkness, but rather reprove them."*[a]

We learn from John's example that Christians—and most especially Christian leaders—can no longer excuse silence (in calling secular leaders to accountability) by saying, "That is not what we are called to do" or "It is in the hands of the Lord. We will not get involved." That view is simply not biblical.

Our corporate refusal to lead in both the spiritual and secular realms leaves the world open to corrupt guidance.

Toward the end of the twentieth century, the world experienced unparalleled family disintegration, terror of an unharnessed AIDS epidemic, famines of epic proportions and horrendous ethnic cleansing. No world body (apart from one led by God) can eradicate these killers because these problems originate in the sinful heart of man. Ultimately, only God

[a]Ephesians 5:11

can change the human heart. Until that change takes place, Christians (who live the beliefs they espouse) have the only foundation to provide the ethical leadership every nation needs to curtail human misery and destruction.

The question we must ask is this: "How can believers in Jesus Christ bring help and light to a hurting world, yet still be responsible in secular affairs of government (including holding governmental officials answerable for their performances)?"

CHAPTER 2

FOUNDING FATHERS REVEAL DEMOCRACY'S STRENGTH

During the twentieth century (as Christians argued and splintered into innumerable divisions over non-essential doctrines), a seemingly innocuous idea slipped into our culture. Its damage was immeasurable. This concept—which we hear bandied about so often it seems true—is that the founding fathers established "separation of church and state." I've watched this false notion of separation develop into a determined push to eradicate public reference to God, memorials of His achievements, discussion of belief in the workplace and all prayer (except inside homes or churches).

This cliché of separation was pulled from the First Amendment to the Constitution. This First Amendment on a list of ten (known as The Bill of Rights) begins, "Congress shall make no law respecting an establishment of religion or prohibiting the free exercise thereof." An objective person can plainly see these words do not build a wall of separation between religion and the state, but rather assure us that the government will never mandate a state religion (such as was done in the European countries from where our founding fathers came).

To obtain accurate understanding of the First Amendment, a sincere searcher would examine other writings by the authors of the Bill of Rights to discover their intent. The writings of Fisher Ames are important because he was the congressman from Massachusetts who **suggested the wording of the First Amendment**. I discovered he most certainly believed in Christianity's integration into secular government. This was evidenced by his comment about public education. Concerning teaching our children, he stated, "Should not the Bible regain the place it once held as a schoolbook? Its morals are pure, its examples are captivating and noble"..."by teaching all the same they will speak alike, and the Bible will justly remain the standard of language as well as of faith."[2]

The total respect and familiarity the founding fathers had of the Bible was demonstrated by the fact that ninety-four percent of the quotes in their writings came from the Bible. [3]

The signature on the original proposal for the Bill of Rights is that of John Adams, then Vice-President under George Washington. It becomes evident from Adams' writings just how "separated" the church and state were intended to be and just how much mix there was of religion and politics. He wrote, "Our Constitution was made for a moral and religious people. It is wholly inadequate to the government of any other"[4] and that "religion and virtue are the only foundations, not only of republicanism and of all free government, but of social felicity under all governments and in the combinations of human society." [5]

Note when "religion" is discussed, the framers of our government were **not** speaking of all beliefs that might gather under the umbrella of religion. They were quite specific. Adams states in his diary, "The Christian religion is above all the religions that ever prevailed or existed in ancient or modern times." [6]

On July 4, 1821, John Quincy Adams, sixth President of the United States, announced, "The highest glory of the American Revolution was this; it connected in one indissoluble bond the principles of civil government with the principles of Christianity." [7]

Signer of the Declaration of Independence and father of public schools, Benjamin Rush, declared, "The only foundation for...a republic is to be laid in Religion. Without this there can be no virtue and without virtue there can be no liberty."[8]

America's first President, George Washington, asked, "Where is the security of property, for reputation, for life, if the sense of religious obligation desert?...Let us with caution indulge the supposition that morality can be maintained without religion."[9]

United States Supreme Court Justice Joseph Story superbly clarified the original meaning of the First Amendment. (Justice Story's words were quoted by Judge Brevard Hand in the Alabama courts in 1983.) "The original object of the First Amendment was not to countenance, much less to advance Mohammedanism, or Judaism, or infidelity, by prostrating Christianity, but to exclude all rivalry among Christian sects [denominations] and to prevent any national ecclesiastical patronage of the national government." [10]

Research shows that **the first official act of Congress was to open in prayer**. [So much for the myth of separation of church and state!]

Jesus spoke of dual citizenship when He said, "*Render therefore unto Caesar the things which are Caesar's; and unto God the things that are God's."* [a] Note, these familiar words teach the difference in responsibility toward church and state—**not separation of state from God.**

In summarizing the founding fathers' view of religion and politics, Norman Geisler, noted author, lecturer and dean of Southern Evangelical Seminary, gives wise guidelines. In understanding the function of government, he writes, "The very purpose of government is to legislate moral behavior. But it is not the providence of government to regulate religion. We should avoid both a purely secular government or a uniquely religious one and work rather for a just one." [11]

God's instructions in the Romans 13 passage (to pray for our leaders) can't be used to abrogate our duty to ask for—yes, even demand—integrity and accountability from elected officials.

The very Constitution that allows us to

---

[a]Matthew 22:21

select our leaders by casting a vote also gives provision for removing unqualified officeholders by the impeachment process. **If it is a moral and Christian act to vote, then it is a moral and Christian act to call for impeachment if necessary**. The call for impeachment cannot be made unless those who believe in accountability, who possess an ethical anchor and who stand for integrity, provide essential specific facts to the American people.

John Adams, the second President of the United States, believed in pastors calling all people to accountability, whether they were in government or not. "It is the duty of the clergy to accommodate their discourses to the times...If the rights and duties of Christian magistrates and subjects are disputed, should they not explain them, show their nature, ends, limitations, and restrictions." [12]

July 4th brings thoughts of picnics and fireworks, but remember, it is a benchmark day of American history. We commemorate the time in 1776 when our founding fathers signed the Declaration of Independence. This document, outlining the moral reasons for the independence of the United States of America, continues today to impact the world with its wisdom. Once again, while reading in this landmark manuscript, I marveled that the power of government, given by God, is a "self-evident" truth. It also states, "To secure these rights, governments are instituted among men, deriving their just powers from the consent of the governed...But when a long train of abuses and usurpations, pursuing invariably the same object, evinces a design to reduce them under absolute despotism, it is their right, it is their duty to throw off such government and to provide new guards for their future security."

The Declaration continues by listing twenty-eight grievances (against their authorized political leader, the King) including: "He has erected a multitude of new offices, and sent out hither swarms of officers to harass our people, and to eat out their substance" and "for taking away our charters, abolishing our most valuable laws, and altering, fundamentally, the powers of our government."

In the conclusion of the Declaration, we see that the frustration of the founding fathers greatly parallels the growing frustration of Americans today—particularly Christians: "In every stage of these oppressions, we have petitioned for redress, in the most humble terms; our repeated petitions have been answered only by repeated injury. A prince, whose character is thus marked by every act which may define a tyrant, is unfit to be the ruler of a free people."

Today, we must still measure each government representative by those words from The Declaration of Independence by asking, "Is this leader fit to rule a free people?"

Benjamin Franklin demonstrated exactly how and why the United States came into being when he proposed the motto for a seal that would capture the spirit of the new United States. He composed the words, **"Rebellion to tyrants is obedience to God."** [13]

CHAPTER 3

GODLY LEADERS IN BIBLICAL TIMES

The dilemma in which we Christians find ourselves is certainly not new. We have always been faced with dividing our efforts, time and allegiances between both worlds of which we are citizens.

I was impressed by the challenge of the great American preacher, Charles G. Finney: "The church must take right ground in regards to politics...The time has come for Christians to vote for honest men, and take consistent ground in politics or the Lord will curse them...**Politics are a part of religion in such a country as this**, and Christians must do their duty to their country as a part of their duty to God...**God will bless or curse this nation according to the course Christians take in politics."**[14] (emphasis mine)

Since we Christians use the Bible to guide our lives, let's look at five instances when followers of God delivered harsh messages to political leaders, demanding their repentance.

1. Moses presented the Pharaoh of Egypt a message of God's potential doom. Moses had many of the same doubts that we might have today. He showed reluctance in calling a secular leader to task, but he did it anyway. Sadly, Pharaoh didn't repent, so through Moses, God implemented the exodus which freed the nation of Israel from slavery.

2. King Ahab and his wife Jezebel were perhaps the most wicked pair to ever rule Israel. Notice that when the prophet Elijah, who spoke boldly against the sin in the lives of both his king and

queen, Elijah is accused of "troubling Israel." Ahab, instead of taking responsibility for the trials in Israel brought on by his own corrupt leadership, blames the man of God who dares to call him a "sinner."

Elijah didn't let that ploy of Ahab deter him one bit in the delivery of his message. He instead drew the original line in the sand when he said to the people, *"How long will ye halt between two opinions?"*[a] Elijah risked the wrath of this fierce king in order to be God's faithful messenger.

3. Familiar to many is the sin of King David. He committed adultery with Bathsheba, which resulted in her

[a] I Kings 18:17-21

becoming pregnant. Then, when he couldn't arrange for the woman's husband to have a conjugal visit with her, David asked his faithful military captain Joab to arrange the death of the husband. David was a popular king, loved by his people, but he sinned gravely. One man, Nathan the prophet, obeyed God and confronted King David with the multiple sins he had committed. Nathan dared to call this otherwise faithful and brave king to task for his sin.

4. God used Jonah to warn a violent heathen city, Nineveh, about impending judgment from God. The inhabitants and the king of this imposing city (capital of the Assyrian empire) became convicted of

their sins and repented, asking God to forgive them. He did.

Amazingly, for selfish reasons, Jonah hadn't wanted to deliver that message to the sinners of his day. He hated the Ninevites and was afraid they might repent! How odd. Today these motives are reversed. Christians hesitate to deliver what could be called "God's ultimatum" to the sinners in our capital city, because **not condemning is perceived as the loving thing to do!**

5. The perfect example of a faithful believer delivering a message of "repent or be judged" lies in the book of Daniel. Nebuchadnezzar, king of the Babylonian empire, was

warned by Daniel to repent of his sins or lose his empire. The king refused, then lost his rulership. Happily, he later repented, and God restored his position.

Four of the five leaders whom God's people criticized in these examples were not believers, **but still they were held accountable to the Lord for their earthly rule**. I'm encouraged to note that because of the faithful and bold witness of believers, three out of the five leaders repented, two coming to faith in God for the first time!

CHAPTER 4

PROBLEM LEADERSHIP: HOW TO REACT

Our response to any evil leadership must be biblical, whether the leader is a local politician or the President of the United States. I chose to examine the dilemma of just how involved a Christian should become in secular politics (and whether or not one should actively speak out against ungodly leaders) by using the example of a high-profile politician from the late twentieth century. For quite some time this man needed to be called into accountability, and his leadership begged to be examined in light of the Scriptures.

Many twentieth century political figures led lives reeking from habitual ethical infractions, but my choice was the well-documented example of the paradoxical President—Bill Clinton. He was first elected to office in 1992 and soon became the classic case of a man rising to power, going too long without accountability for his actions.

Before his nomination, the problem areas of this forty-second President's life were not known by most residents of the U.S. The first red flag that alerted biblically discerning Christians was Clinton's use of the Holy Scriptures. His acceptance speech at the Democratic National Convention contained the following: *"Eye hath not yet seen nor our ears heard, nor our minds imagined what we can build."* His promise was a corrupt rewrite of I Corinthians 2:9, *"Eye hath not seen, nor ear heard, neither have entered into the heart of man, the things which God hath prepared for them that love him."* Clinton's misdeeds, his anti-biblical choice of leaders and his rewriting of scripture continued into his presidency, bringing the Christian's dual citizenship into sharp focus. All this caused many (including me) to seek the correct biblical response to corrupt leadership.

The ease with which Clinton was able to appoint leaders who supported guidelines that shredded the very fabric of a once biblically-based nation demonstrated the results of Christian apathy in the political arena. The Bible records God's demand that rulers must be accountable to Him. God warns political leaders by saying, *"The kings of the earth set themselves, and the rulers take counsel together, against the LORD...Be wise now therefore, O ye kings: be instructed, ye judges of the earth. Serve the LORD with fear."* [a] Again God declares, "*Woe unto them that decree unrighteous decrees.*" As discerning American people observed the true character of the person they elected President in 1992, they discovered Bill Clinton to be one of those leaders who "*set themselves...against the Lord*" and "*decree unrighteous decrees.*"[b]

Had the media been even moderately honest in its coverage of candidates before the Democratic Convention, I believe the

---

[a]Psalm 2:2,10-11

[b]Isaiah 10:1

delegates would not have chosen Clinton for their 1992 presidential candidate. Even after his nomination, had the multiplicity of hidden elements in Clinton's life been understood by the voters at large, I would hope that Americans never would have elected him President. Unfortunately, the largely-liberal media withheld facts from the public concerning Clinton's alleged criminal behavior as well as his well-publicized deviant, sexual promiscuity.

Long before Bill Clinton ran for President, people who knew firsthand (and had proof) of his amoral lifestyle and criminal activity tried in vain to make their information known. Sadly, the spin-doctoring and personal attacks against those who tried to present the truth provided barriers too formidable to overcome.

It wasn't until 1994 that those injured by Clinton (and who possessed damaging information about his illegal and immoral way of life) finally became successful in exposing truth and bringing this dire situation to the attention of the American people. Numerous Christian and conservative action groups were formed to correct the doctored information and promote truth. My part in bringing the facts out was to form Citizens For Honest Government and to produce the video and book, *The Clinton Chronicles.* Only a portion of the information that linked Clinton to potentially criminal activity was presented in the film and book; yet even that portion revealed an alarming number of ethical and moral lapses of Bill Clinton. Those projects, in concert with conservative radio programs and patriotic newsletters, informed the public, who in turn urged Congress to investigate the dangerous propensities of President Clinton. Although at first the mainstream media ignored or covered up these allegations, the demands of the American people eventually forced them to bring some truth to light.

Choosing Bill Clinton as an example

of a corrupt leader who should be held accountable for his actions is not a partisan attack. His violations simply were the most flagrant of any U.S. leader. When I first became involved in alerting Americans to the severity and extent of Clinton's sordid leadership, Christian friends suggested keeping quiet. They said, "Look, none of us are without fault. Now that Clinton is President, we should support him as best we can. The Bible says all powers are ordained of God. Pray for him, submit to his leadership and, who knows, in time, with our prayers, maybe he'll come around."

I considered that reasoning, consulted the Bible and concluded that I must actively pursue a course of exposing Clinton's deeds and asking the American people, particularly Christians, to do the same. Just to let you know what kind of information prompted my decision, I must list the litany of offenses in Bill Clinton's life as well as the well-documented allegations against him, either of which should have disqualified him as a candidate for the office of President. I will also present the scriptures which influenced me.

- Before becoming Governor of Arkansas, Bill Clinton:

  1. wrote to a colonel (a veteran of WW II and Korea) that he "loathes the military",
  2. lied to avoid serving in the military,
  3. actively organized and led protests against our Armed Forces,
  4. supported the military cause of communist regimes,
  5. admitted he possessed and smoked an illegal drug,
  6. established a lifestyle of sexual unrestraint (in methods and numbers) that made mainstream Americans ashamed.

- After being elected Governor, Clinton:

    1. illegally channeled taxpayers' money to his campaigns and wife's business associates,
    2. pardoned good friend Dan Lasater from his conviction of distributing cocaine to minors,
    3. made felonious use of Arkansas tax money to finance his sexual liaisons,
    4. purposely consorted with people known to be involved in criminal activity,
    5. began the crime of "obstruction of justice" by destroying incriminating evidence, and
    6. adopted the method of "buying off" witnesses who threatened to come forward to tell the truth about his corruption.

Clinton's past contained so many blots that it's highly unlikely he could have passed an FBI background check for a security clearance even to work as a White House janitor!

In light of the growing number of witnesses who were willing to give first-hand testimony about Clinton's corruption, and in view of the seriousness of the allegations, it's hard to imagine that any Americans, especially Christians, could have been indifferent to the charges once they learned about them.

Let me give an example closer to home: If you were the parent of a young child and became aware of documented information that your Little League coach (who also sang in your church choir) was involved in criminal activities, drug dealing, and, as a married man, regularly cheated on his wife with a variety of women, should you say, "Leave him alone. Let him coach. After all, what does a man's private life have to do with the way he coaches our child?"

Of course not. As a responsible parent you would respond by reporting the coach's behavior to the proper authorities, not letting the issue rest until he proved his innocence or was found guilty.

Should anyone treat the office of the President of the United States as less important than that of a Little League coach?

Some rebutted the whole idea of questioning Clinton's qualifications to serve as President by saying, "No one, and certainly no politician, is without his gray areas. Most great Presidents had a mistress or a few flings, so why make a big deal out of Clinton's indulgences?"

In answer, be aware that only lately have revisionist historians tried to stretch obscure passages in early history books to insinuate that most of the founding fathers of America were habitual adulterers.[15] It appears that these pseudo-historians are simply trying to justify the sordid lives of their own current political icons.

Furthermore, if anyone does know leaders (secular or religious) who tell their constituents to lead lives of honesty and commitment, but regularly fail to do so themselves, the informed person has a responsibility to speak up. **Tolerance toward diversity is good; tolerance toward sin is deadly.**

American voters should have examined Bill Clinton's known character and the well-documented allegations against him. It was more than just a few "flings" that we should have been concerned about.

Clinton's life and record as Governor of Arkansas amply demonstrated the amoral legacy he would be bringing to the White House in 1992. His past performance gave telling insight as to how he would perform as President. Look at his record.

- In only his first two years as President, Bill Clinton:

    1. appointed over thirty open homosexuals and lesbians to high Cabinet positions,

2. selected and continued to support cabinet members who supported teaching all school children detailed information on how to "do" sex and described sexual "variety" with same-sex partners as being wholesome for our children,
3. headed a staff which continually helped cover his past by shredding and destroying incriminating documents,
4. appointed people involved in illegal activities to high-level positions in the White House Cabinet,
5. advocated forcing the military to accept homosexuals and lesbians, even against advice from top military leaders,
6. ordered our military to fight a doomed war of social engineering in Somalia,
7. orchestrated a military invasion,

in spite of public and congressional disapproval (against third-world Haiti), in order to replace a military dictator with an "elected" socialist terrorist,

8. persisted in maligning, demoralizing and dismantling our armed forces,
9. continued to "redefine" both the government and the military to fit socialist and globalist guidelines and agenda,
10. pushed through legislation (Freedom of Access to Clinic Entrances Act) which unfairly targeted and penalized those who protest against the killing of unborn babies,
11. literally redefined God's definition of "family", supporting anti-family legislation, such as allowing same-sex adoptions and recognizing same-sex marriages.

12. adjusted income thresholds, causing higher taxes for couples who marry,
13. supported EEOC legislation that would have encouraged officials under the guise of "equal opportunity employment" to make it a crime to speak of God in the workplace,
14. played on people's fear of crime to push through a pork-barrel crime bill that in reality was another social program, one which put him in charge of dispensing billions of dollars at his discretion,
15. appointed leaders and supported legislation that elevated alleged needs of plants, animals and the environment over the needs of human beings,
16. promoted Outcome Based Education (OBE) school curriculum through Goals 2000,

which uses a multicultural, holistic, no grades and no grade-level system,

17. bowed to the homosexual lobby by seeking to lift the ban on admitting immigrants with AIDS, and
18. continued (along with his staff) to be caught in numerous lies in attempts to hide illegal and immoral activities.

The question we as Christians need to consider is this: "What is the proper biblical course to take when we recognize blatant, recurring sin and abuse of power in the life of a leader of our country?" While in this quest, I was mindful that God is the ultimate judge. We must never usurp His authority by gossiping or speaking evil of dignities. He also warns us to *"never accuse anyone falsely."*[a]

Open and honest hearings into allegations against leaders is absolutely

[a]Luke 3:14

necessary, to either verify charges or vindicate the accused.

Sincere Christians understand that God teaches us to pray for all those who are in authority over us.[a] Our family does that and we encourage others to do the same. We should all pray regularly and specifically for the President, his cabinet members, our Congress and our local and state officials. We must pray that their decisions will be wise, that they will lead our country in a way that would help the American people and would honor God; we also need to pray that each one of them will come to know Jesus Christ as their Savior.

[a]Romans 13:1-7; I Timothy 2:1-4

CHAPTER 5

PRACTICAL BIBLICAL SOLUTIONS

Still, even among those who recognized Bill Clinton's leadership and life as ungodly, there were some who hesitated to criticize him, believing that resisting his leadership would have been *"resisting the ordinance of God."* They perceived this prohibition to be in the Romans 13 passage. *"Let every soul be subject unto the higher powers. For there is no power but of God: the powers that be are ordained of God. Whosoever therefore resisteth the power, resisteth the ordinance of God: Wherefore ye must needs be subject...For for this cause pay ye tribute also: for they are God's ministers."*

These verses could mean that all persons in positions of leadership are chosen and placed there by God. Although the primary focus of this passage is somewhat different, Scripture does indicate that God controls promotion.[a] But a careful reading of this whole section shows that the main thrust of this passage is focused on government, not on those who govern. Christians must not resist the **institution of government**. God clarifies the focus when he mentions the Christian's responsibility to pay taxes as an example of submission to government.

Again we are told to *"Submit yourselves to every ordinance of man for the Lord's sake: whether it be to the king, as supreme; Or unto governors, as unto them that are sent by him for the punishment of evildoers, and for the praise of them that do well. For so is the will of God, that with well doing ye may put to silence the ignorance of foolish men."*[b]

In both instances we are directed to be law-abiding citizens so that our testimony among unbelievers will not be marred. However, as astutely noted by theologian Donald Grey Barnhouse in his

[a]Psalm 75:6-7

[b]I Peter 2:13-15

commentary on Romans, the very description of the government in the Romans passage defines the leadership: *"For rulers are **not a terror to good works, but to the evil."*** Also note the First Peter passage describes a government sent ***"for the punishment of evildoers, and for the praise of them that do well."***

It becomes a leap in logic to say that if God ordains all leaders then we must support them all, no matter what policies they institute. To the contrary, these and hundreds of other verses tell us to hold leaders accountable.

Let's grant for a moment that the recent observation of a leading evangelical was correct. He wrote, "I needed to relate to him [Clinton] not on the basis of my opinion, but on the basis that his presidency was appointed by God." This pastor continues by comparing Abraham Lincoln to Hitler. Although, as he points out, one brought goodness to his country and the other brought destruction, "Both came to office under the sovereign will of God." God does bring people to power, but we must also recognize that **nowhere in the Scriptures are we told to keep a leader** who goes directly against the mandates of God.

If we make the assumption that leaders occupy a "hands off" position, we box ourselves into an impossible corner. You see, according to Scripture, **anyone** who possesses power does so under the permissive will of God. The Bible states, *"Power belongeth unto God."*[a] Even Satan, the Prince of the Power of the Air, has no power except that allowed him by God, but does it follow that we must be passive and not resist Satan? Does that mean that we should sit idly by as the Devil destroys unsuspecting lives because we don't want to *"resist the ordinance of God?"* Of course not. God tells us to "resist" Satan.

Does it follow that if a pastor or a town mayor is involved in drug running, regularly

---

[a]Psalm 62:11

commits adultery and is siphoning money from the people and putting it into his own pocket, we should not ask him to step down because God gave them the office? Again, of course not. Let's summarize the thrust of the Romans 13 message:

1. The offices of leadership and government are ordained of God.

2. Leaders are to be obeyed and followed **only as long as they are not a terror to good works, but to the evil.**

As we recall the list of Bill Clinton's proven deeds (forget the allegations for a moment), has he been *"not a terror to good works?"* Has he been sent for the *"punishment of evildoers, and praise of them that do well?"*

The correct understanding of these scriptures clearly condemns the Christians in Nazi Germany who stood by with folded hands while the godless leaders persecuted, and then exterminated, "undesirable" people groups and "useless eaters." Inaction by those passive Christians cannot be justified by a supposed desire to respect a *"God-ordained"* leader. History reveals that these Christians compromised their witness, failing to speak out against Hitler because they thought their own churches and personal freedoms might be jeopardized if they did. After all, Hitler "said" he was Christian and he "said" he wanted to support Christianity. In time, the Christians found themselves being killed by Hitler anyway.

In spite of the example of Hitler's betrayal of Christians, believers in America are making the same mistake today. We support politicians based on their words and their image in the media, disregarding their actions. Remember, in politics, one cannot rise too high without developing the fine art of using words skillfully. Knowledge of a politician's skill must prompt us to even more carefully evaluate leaders by biblical guidelines.

What are those guidelines? God says to judge people by their fruit—it's not what people say that counts, it's what they do.

Those scriptures in Romans and First Peter cannot be used to teach that all government leaders are good, that they must always be obeyed and that they are never to be questioned. Leaders must first qualify as "not a terror to good works." Peter demonstrated this premise of **not** submitting yourselves to every ordinance of man whenever the leader or the ordinance is against God's Word. When local officials warned Peter not to teach using the name of Jesus, he announced, *"We ought to obey God rather than men."*[a]

After Paul's arrest in Jerusalem he appeared before the governor of Judea, Felix, and his wife Drusella. Internationally-

[a]Acts 5:29

loved Bible teacher Harry Ironside wrote that history shows Felix to be "a most unprincipled man, an ungodly, scheming politician who stooped often to the very lowest of methods in order to bring about his purposes." Felix often called a special group of assassins "who were pledged to undertake to destroy anyone for whose death they were paid."[16] Felix took Drusella from her husband, married her, and the two carried on as partners in sin and corruption.

Interestingly, when Paul testified before Felix the first time, Scripture indicates Felix had prior knowledge of the gospel. The second time Paul appeared before Felix, the message was one of sin and judgment. Evidently the words Paul spoke were extremely strong because "Felix trembled." Paul demonstrated his love toward Felix and Drusella by telling them the truth. He warned them about their sin and God's impending judgment upon them.[a]

[a]Acts 24:22-25

Both Peter and Paul chose when to speak kindly to leaders, when to resist leaders and when to call them to task.

Somewhere in this century we lost our focus on how to deliver the gospel to people in high places. The message to all people great and small is the same: You are a sinner and lost in your sins. But God loves you, and has provided a way of salvation. Confess, repent and ask Jesus to be your Lord and Savior. If a hearer is convicted and prays for forgiveness and Salvation, we can only hope that their heart is truly repentant. In time (and this is the only key we have to presume to gauge their sincerity), if the experience was genuine, we will see the fruit of the Spirit in their lives. Again, we must believe their lives above their words.

CHAPTER 6

CONFUSION IN THE RANKS: MIXED MESSAGES

How well did the Christian community address the problem leadership of Bill Clinton? Some members called for accountability. They braved the epitaphs thrown at them from the liberal ranks of "religion." Any time obedient Christians dare to step forward and proclaim the fact that God has standards that are absolute, opposition is to be expected. Especially when violations of these standards are called sin (and the violators are called sinners), screams go up of "narrow-minded", "judgmental", and "unloving." This satanic ploy is familiar.

Although it was no surprise to be called "bigot" or "hate monger" because a few of us dared to ask the top leader of our nation to account for his cornucopia of lies, it did produce a deep sadness to hear some of these negative appellations come from the mouths of fellow evangelicals. As mentioned before, most people would examine serious allegations made against their local leaders. Why then wouldn't Christians examine (and care about) the allegations against President Clinton, **especially when he classified himself as a minister of God**? Note well his words of August 15, 1994, spoken from the pulpit of the Full Gospel AME Zion Church: **"Our ministry is to do the work of God here on earth."**

Some Christians still felt they should not speak in criticism against President Clinton. The following list represents their reasoning:

1. "You can not full-heartedly, compassionately or power-fully pray for a person unless you love him."

In answer, we say, "Godly love should prompt not only prayer, it should also prompt us to warn sinners about the consequences of not turning from their sins." Love for a person or a generation of people mandates that we deliver a true message.

Look at the dire message of judgment delivered by Enoch, aimed at the generation which would experience the Coming of Jesus. *"Behold, the Lord cometh with ten thousands of his saints, to execute judgment upon all, and to convince all that are ungodly among them of all their ungodly deeds which they have ungodly committed"* [a] That was a horrific message of judgment Enoch delivered to mankind, but **God seemed pleased with Enoch's demeanor**. In fact, the Bible describes Enoch in a uniquely spiritual way, saying, "*Enoch walked with God: and he was not; for God took him.*"[b]

2. "We are instructed to pray for those in authority over us."

[a]Jude 1:14-16

[b]Genesis 5:24

Our reply is, "Of course we must and we do pray for all those in leadership. However, that does not in any way hinder us from seeking accountability or asking habitually incompetent or wicked leaders to step aside until their values and actions are in order."

3. "It's not loving to criticize. In fact, criticism of Clinton constitutes intolerance and hate."

This objection sounds like the rhetoric coming from the homosexual lobbies, the ACLU and the pro-abortionists when anyone suggests that God's laws are absolute. Jesus criticized false leaders quite harshly. Was He full of hate? Was Jesus not loving when He addressed social and spiritual ills of the first century? Notice, He even called fellow religious leaders "vipers" and compared them with "whitewashed sepulchers, full of dead men's bones."[a] Was Jesus "hate mongering" when he described the confrontational aspects of His redemptive agenda as "bringing a sword"?[a]

4. "The President's personal life and character are irrelevant."

We reply, "How sad it is when Christians adopt the reasoning Joe Klein wrote about in *Newsweek*: 'It can be persuasively argued that a politician's private life gives no indication of his or her ability to perform public duties.'"[17] If Klein's observation is accurate, why do even the lowest security clearances for the government and the military involve **checking a person's reputation and character**?

What does the Bible say about character?[b] *"Even a child is known by his doings, whether his work be pure, and whether it be right."* Again God says, *"I the*

---

[a]Matthew 23:27

[a]Matthew 10:34

[b]Proverbs 20:11

LORD search the heart, I try the reins, even to give every man according to his ways, and according to the fruit of his doings."[a]

If Bill Clinton is a "struggling believer", as he stated on ABC's World News Tonight, or "an evangelical Christian who wants to be religious" (as Clinton was described by a Christian leader writing in *Bookstore Journal*, January 1994), then his sordid life and continued cover-ups become even greater infractions. Leaders must be held to a standard of honesty and integrity, and Christian leaders even more so. According to God, not many should presume to lead others because of this higher level of responsibility. "*My brethren, be not many masters, knowing that we shall receive the greater condemnation.*"[b]

Christian leaders confuse not only the people they lead when they fail to confront instances of immoral leadership, they also muddy the gospel message. Individuals

---

[a]Jeremiah 17:10

[b]James 3:1

who haven't yet faced their sinfulness will not feel the need for salvation. In fact, toward the end of the twentieth century, the false message of inherent "self" goodness had so permeated American society that people being presented with the good news of salvation sometimes responded with "saved from what?" [18]

The message of judgment for sin is an intregal part of the gospel.

True love confronts with the truth.

CHAPTER 7

GODLY APPLICATION OF OUR EARTHLY CITIZENSHIP

What then should the biblical response be when the leadership of a nation becomes a *"terror to good works?"* As we examine the scriptures which shed light on this question, remember that Bill Clinton, my example of a leader who must be called to task, was not only an elected servant of the people, but he also categorized himself as an evangelical Christian. The Bible gives us information on how to handle unjust leaders who are not believers, and it gives us **an even stricter set of guidelines** for handling sinning leaders who are professed believers. The guidelines from God that show us how to biblically deal with Clinton also can be used to regulate our response toward other politicians showing moral or ethical lapses.

Since Clinton's previously listed agenda obviously <u>is</u> a terror to good works, we must, as God says, *"warn them that are unruly."*[a] That is a Christian's duty. The Bible also teaches the local church to deal strongly with any believers who live in overt sin, by disassociating with them.[b] We must not in good conscience refer to Bill Clinton as a man of God, nor praise his choice of cabinet members, nor suggest he served the Lord as evidenced by the multiplied ungodly decisions he made as President.

The seriousness of exposing the misdeeds of my own President brought many sleepless nights. Once, near dawn, after seeking the Lord's guidance, I opened a daily devotional written by Dr. Bill Bright and read the next day's Scripture text. The words burned in my heart. God stated, *"Hear the word at my mouth, and give them warning from me. When I say unto the wicked, Thou shalt surely die; and thou givest him not warning, nor speakest to warn the wicked from his wicked way, to save his life; the same wicked man shall die*

---

[a]I Thessalonians 5:14

[b]I Corinthians 5:1-5

in his iniquity; but his blood will I require at thine hand."[a]

Christian leader, you have a responsibility. God's Word gives a sobering warning to religious leaders who *"speak a vision of their own heart, and not out of the mouth of the LORD. They say still unto them that despise me, The LORD hath said, Ye shall have peace; and they say unto every one that walketh after the imagination of his own heart, No evil shall come upon you."*[b] For any religious leader to assure Bill Clinton that he is God's man for the hour—just because he was elected—does Clinton no service, does our country no favor and certainly is condemned by that scripture.

A more biblical description of Clinton, who claims to be a Christian, might be: "*For there are many unruly and vain talkers and deceivers...Unto the pure all things are pure: but unto them that are defiled and*

[a]Ezekiel 3:17-18

[b]Jeremiah 23:16-17

unbelieving is nothing pure; but even their mind and conscience is defiled. They profess that they know God; but in works they deny him, being abominable, and disobedient, and unto every good work reprobate...A man that is an heretic after the first and second admonition reject; Knowing that he that is such is subverted, and sinneth, being condemned of himself."[a]

As Christian spokespersons, we must all, *"Take heed therefore unto yourselves, and to all the flock, over the which the Holy Ghost hath made you overseers, to feed the church of God, which he hath purchased with his own blood."*[b] If Christian leaders do not speak out against the evil agenda of our government and if they fail to teach their flocks to recognize evil leadership—even if it means calling the President of the United States to accountability—then the Scripture might

[a]Titus 1:10,15-16; 3:10-11

[b]Acts 20:28

well take effect, *"Therefore thus saith the LORD God of Israel against the pastors that feed my people; Ye have scattered my flock, and driven them away, and have not visited them: behold, I will visit upon you the evil of your doings."* [a]

God tells Christians what to do. We must because of the grace of God, *"deny ungodliness and worldly lusts."* We ourselves *"should live soberly, righteously, and godly, in this present world;"* as well as *"speak, and exhort, and* ***rebuke with all authority****."* [b]

Positive Steps

Harriet Beecher Stowe served as a schoolteacher but became famous for her soul-stirring book, *Uncle Tom's Cabin.* She took the personal risk to speak up about the legal but ungodly issue of her day. Her classic work greatly touched the American people. She dared to write about the

---

[a]Jeremiah 23:2

[b]Titus 2:10-15

abolition of slavery. The impact of her work caused President Lincoln to greet her by saying, "So you're the little lady who started the big war." She ends her monumental book by warning, "A day of grace is yet held out to us. Both North and South have been guilty before God; and the Christian church has a heavy account to answer. Not by combining together, to protect injustice and cruelty, and making a common capital of sin, is this Union to be saved, but by repentance, justice and mercy." [19]

Today, we the people of the United States also have a choice. We can acknowledge that from the lowest to the highest offices in the land, character does count. We can stop selecting leaders on the shallow basis of their charm or their promises, but on the solid basis of their established record of performance and their character. We must stop supporting or even voting for candidates who are the "lesser of two evils." Evil is still evil. We must not be afraid to ask leaders to either be accountable or to step down. We must seek out leaders whose lives fit this list of God's qualifications. "*He that walketh righteously, and speaketh uprightly; he that despiseth the gain of oppressions, that shaketh his hands from holding of bribes, that stoppeth his ears from hearing of blood, and shutteth his eyes from seeing evil.*"[a]

Fellow Christians: Let us step forward and once again assume positions of leadership in our country, our media, our arts, our education, our industry and our politics. The choice belongs to us. "*Thus saith the LORD; Behold, I set before you the way of life, and the way of death.*"[b]

No one (whether Christian or not) should be exempt from behaving responsibly, especially leaders. Even King David was held accountable for his sins, and God used a religious leader to call him to task. During Hitler's rule of terror, Christian leaders Bonhoffer and Neimoeller

---

[a]Isaiah 33:15

[b]Jeremiah 21:8

were imprisoned for their stand against Hitler. Bonhoffer died for this commitment. We must stand as did they. We can do no less.

There is hope for our country, and that hope is spiritual. God says, *"If **my** people, which are called by my name, shall humble themselves, and pray, and seek my face, and turn from their wicked ways; then will I hear from heaven, and will forgive their sin, and will heal their land."*[a]

We must not lose hope. The example of John Quincy Adams speaks loudly to us at this time. He opposed slavery in an era when Congress even forbade discussion on of the issue. "When asked why he never seemed discouraged or depressed over championing such an unpopular fight, Adams replied:

'Duty is ours; results are God's.'"[20]

[a]II Chronicles 7:14

ENDNOTES

1.Federer, William F., *America's God and Country*, Coppell, TX:FAME Publishing, Inc. 1994, pp. 256, 257

2.Ibid. p. 26

3.Ibid. p. 49

4.Ibid. pp. 10, 11

5.Ibid. pp. 10, 11

6.Ibid. p. 10

7.Ibid. p. 18

8.*Wallbuilders*, Summer 1993, p. 3

9.Ibid. p. 2

10.Ibid. p. 25

11.Geisler, Norman L., *Fundamentalist Journal*, July/August 1988, p. 64

12.Ibid. p. 8

13.Ibid. p. 245

14.Ibid. p. 235

15.Millard, Catherine, *The Rewriting of America's History*, Horizon House Publishers, Camp Hill, Pennsylvania, 1991

16.Ironside, H. A., *Acts* (Neptune, NJ: Loizeaux Brothers, Inc. 1943), pp. 577-578

17.Klein, Joe, *Newsweek,* May 9, 1994, p. 16

18.Comfort, Ray, *Hell's Best Kept Secret* (Whitaker House)

19.Ibid. p. 575

20.Federer op. cit. p. 15